First World War
and Army of Occupation
War Diary
France, Belgium and Germany

61 DIVISION
Divisional Troops
Divisional Signal Company
1 December 1915 - 6 June 1916

WO95/3049/1

The Naval & Military Press Ltd
www.nmarchive.com
Published in association with The National Archives

Published by

The Naval & Military Press Ltd

Unit 10 Ridgewood Industrial Park,

Uckfield, East Sussex,

TN22 5QE England

Tel: +44 (0) 1825 749494

www.naval-military-press.com

www.nmarchive.com

This diary has been reprinted in facsimile from the original. Any imperfections are inevitably reproduced and the quality may fall short of modern type and cartographic standards.

© Crown Copyright

Images reproduced by permission of The National Archives, London, England, 2015.

Contents

Document type	Place/Title	Date From	Date To
Heading	WO95/3049/1 Divisional Signal Company		
Heading	61st Division Divl Signal Coy R.E 1915 Dec-1916 Jan (1916 Feb Mar, Apr Diaries Missing)		
Heading	War Diary of 61st Divl. Signal Coy, Royal Engineers, From 1st December 1915 To 31st December 1915 Volume 3		
War Diary	Chelmsford 1/2" O.5	01/12/1915	31/12/1915
Miscellaneous	61st Divl. Signal Coy. R.E.	02/12/1915	02/12/1915
Miscellaneous	61st Divl. Signal Coy. R.E.	16/12/1915	16/12/1915
Heading	War Diary of 61st Divl. Signal Coy. Royal Engineers From 1st January 1916 To 31st January 1916 Volume 4		
War Diary	Chelmsford 1/2" O.S.	01/01/1916	31/01/1916
Miscellaneous	61st Divl. Signal Coy. R.E. Scheme	11/01/1916	11/01/1916
War Diary	Cholderton	01/05/1916	21/05/1916
War Diary	Havre	22/05/1916	24/05/1916
War Diary	St Venant	25/05/1916	31/05/1916
War Diary	In The Field	01/06/1916	01/06/1916
War Diary	St Venant	01/06/1916	06/06/1916

1095/3049 I
Universal Signals Company

61ST DIVISION

DIVL SIGNAL COY R.E.

~~1915 DEC — 1916 JAN~~
~~MAY 1916 — JUN 1919~~
~~ALL~~
~~1916 MAY~~ — 1919 JUN

(1916 FEB, MAR, APR DIARIES MISSING)

C O N F I D E N T I A L.

War Diary of

61st Divl. Signal Coy, Royal Engineers,

from 1st December 1915 to 31st December 1915.

Volume 3.

Page 1
Army Form C. 2118

WAR DIARY
or
INTELLIGENCE SUMMARY

(Erase heading not required.)

61st Divisional Signal Coy R.E.(T)

Instructions regarding War Diaries and Intelligence Summaries are contained in F.S. Regs., Part II. and the Staff Manual respectively. Title Pages will be prepared in manuscript.

Month: December

Place	Date	Hour	Summary of Events and Information	Remarks and references to Appendices
CHELMSFORD ½" O.S.	1-12-15	9.0 am	Authority received to transfer remaining men 1st REINFORCEMENTS 48th Sig Coy to 3rd Line. Cable laying practice and cable repairing.	CJB
CHELMSFORD ½" O.S.	2-12-15	8.30 am	All day scheme. District TILEKILN FM, MARGARETTING, HANNINGFIELD HALL. Pole crossings and hammer jumper work week. Let office work good.	APPENDIX "A" CJB
CHELMSFORD ½" O.S.	3-12-15 — 7-12-15		Company training. Cable laying and repairing all harness and saddlery. All det drums repaired.	CJB
CHELMSFORD ½" O.S.	8-12-15	8.0 am	R det } Experienced kind of laying cable with two wagons. Course from H.Q. 61st SIGNALS L det } to NOAKES FM (Rgt'l ½ O.S. Sheet 36) just over 5 miles laid in 57 minutes. Owing to bad ground (newly ploughed fields) the speed was bad for 2-wagon laying.	CJB
CHELMSFORD ½" O.S.	9-12-15 — 13-12-15		Company training. Cable laying and small "Signal Office" Schemes. Harness all thoroughly inspected by O.C.	CJB
CHELMSFORD ½" O.S.	14-12-15	8.0 am	2nd LIEUT WILLIAMS reported to O.C. for duty. This company. Cable laying (Air line) round Springfield District.	CJB
CHELMSFORD ½" O.S.	15-12-15	8.0 am	Checking stores on wagons and buzzer practice and lecture to Linesmen.	CJB

Page 2
Army Form C. 2118

51st Divisional Signal Coy RE(T)

WAR DIARY
or
INTELLIGENCE SUMMARY
(Erase heading not required.)

Monthly

Place	Date	Hour	Summary of Events and Information	Remarks and references to Appendices
CHELMSFORD ½ "O.S."	16/12/15	8.0 a.m.	All day scheme. District DANBURY — LODDARDS HILL — COLWICKEY GREEN. Main point was that wagons did not start properly equipped. Section Commanders were henceforward to see that they should always make an inspection of their detachment before they start off. Signal Office routine good.	APPENDIX "B" CGB
CHELMSFORD ½ "O.S."	17/12/15	9.30 a.m. 6.0 p.m.	Overhauling wagons after yesterday's scheme. 2nd LIEUT WILLIAMS left for duty with No 3 Brigade Section at BRENTWOOD	CGB
CHELMSFORD ½ "O.S."	18/12/15 19/12/15		Cable repairing & harness cleaning. Veterinary Inspection of horses by Lt OVERS A.V.C.	CGB
CHELMSFORD ½ "O.S."	20/12/15		Arrival of 4th cable wagon but no horses available for it; also a G.S. and 2 pack RE. Company training.	CGB
CHELMSFORD ½ "O.S."	21/12/15 24/12/15	8.0 a.m.	Company training. Infantry drill. Batting Parade and cleaning harness, wagons &c.	CGB
CHELMSFORD ½ "O.S."	25/12/15 26/12/15		Church Parades "	CGB
CHELMSFORD ½ "O.S."	27/12/15 31/12/15		Inventory of all stores in the Company. HQ & No 1 Section and all 3 Brigade Sections. Harness cleaning &c.	CGB

W. Brown Bennett Capt RE
O.C. 51st Divi Sig Coy.

Appendix A

61st Divl. Signal Coy. R.E.

SCHEME - Dec. 2nd 1915.
....

An enemy Force is in position on the line CHIPPING ONGAR - BILLERICAY - WICKFORD, with the intention of capturing CHELMSFORD.

The 61st DIV. at 12.0. noon on Dec. 2nd 1915 is disposed as follows:-

61st DIVL HQS.	TILEKIN FARM S. of MOULSHAM.
182nd BDE HQS.	Cross Roads W. of M in M<u>A</u>RGARETTING.
183rd BDE HQS.	SHIP INN S. of WEST HANNINGFIELD HALL.
184th BDE HQS.	In reserve at DIVL HQS.

At 1.0.p.m. orders will be issued to the BDES. to advance.

PERSONNEL AT DIVL. HQS.
....

G.O.C. 61st DIV.	Capt. J. G. Heaven.
SIGNAL MASTERS.	Lieut. C. E. Bennett.
2nd	" R. J. Spurr.
SIGNAL CLERK	Sergt. A. Meadows.
ASST. SIGNAL CLERK.	Sapper H. E. Aust.
CHECKS.	Sapper C. Burton.
	" W.L. Read.

Signal Clerks will see that Stationery etc. is provided; they will be at DIVL. HQS. by 11.30.a.m.

The BDES. will be represented by:-

182nd BDE.	-	R.H. Detachment.
183rd BDE.	-	L.H. "
184th BDE.	-	H. "
O.C. 182nd BDE.	-	Sergt. Kemshaw.
O.C. 183rd BDE.	-	" Ley.

Appendix B

61st Divl. Signal Coy. R.E.

SCHEME - Dec. 16th 1915.
....

Special Routine Order issued Dec. 16th 15.

6.30.a.m.   Stables.

7.15.a.m.   Breakfast.

8.30.a.m.   Detachments will Parade at their respective Stables and hook in.

9.15.a.m.   Parade outside Signal Coy. Headquarters, Arbour Lane.

SPECIAL INFORMATION.
....

The 61st DIVISION is defending the line SPARR HILL - COLICKEY GREEN.

The positions at noon are as follows:-

DIVL. HQ.   Telegraph Office, DANBURY.

182nd BDE (R).   First D of LODDARDS HILL.

183rd BDE.(L).   N in COLICKEY GREEN.

184th BDE (SR).   (Reserve) OAK INN S of second N in
                              RUNSELL GREEN.

Operation Orders will be issued by G.O.C.

CONFIDENTIAL.

War Diary of

61st Divl. Signal Coy. Royal Engineers.

From 1st January 1916 to 31st January 1916

VOLUME 4.

Army Form C. 2118

WAR DIARY
or
INTELLIGENCE SUMMARY
(Erase heading not required.)

D1st SIGNALS RE Page 1

Instructions regarding War Diaries and Intelligence Summaries are contained in F.S. Regs., Part II. and the Staff Manual respectively. Title Pages will be prepared in manuscript.

Place	Date	Hour	Summary of Events and Information	Remarks and references to Appendices
CHELMSFORD ½" O.S.	1/1/16		Company Instruction.	C.9.B
CHELMSFORD ½" O.S.	2/1/16	5.0 P.M.	CAPT. J.G. HEAVEN O.C. leaves CHELMSFORD to proceed overseas to G.H.Q. B.E.F. for three days instruction under W.O. letter. Lt BENNETT assumes command of the Company.	C.9.B
CHELMSFORD ½" O.S.	3/1/16	9.0 A.M.	Lt WAKE & Lt DICKSON reported here from A.D.A.S. 3RD ARMY for instruction. The Company in special work. Permanent Signal Office fixed up at Room 5 of H.Q.	C.9.B
CHELMSFORD ½" O.S.	4/1/16 7/1/16		Company Instruction. Lectures to Signal Office Staff and H.Q. Telegraph Operators. Instruction in permanent pole climbing. Lectures on lineman duties to linemen & D.Rs. CORPL (M.C.) WHEELER reduced to the ranks for "neglect of duty"	C.9.B
CHELMSFORD ½" O.S.	8/1/16		CAPT. J.G. HEAVEN O.C. returned from B.E.F. and resumed command from this date. Bathing Parades.	C.9.B
CHELMSFORD ½" O.S.	10/1/16		Company Instruction under 3RD ARMY instructors. Lt CLARK reported here from 26° SIGNALS B.E.F. for instructing the Company. 2ND Lt STANTON reported for duty with this company.	C.9.B
CHELMSFORD ½" O.S.	11/1/16		All daytime mainly with the object of instructing H.Q. staff	C.9.B APPENDIX A

Army Form C. 2118

WAR DIARY
or
INTELLIGENCE SUMMARY
(Erase heading not required.)

for 61st SIGNALS R.E.   Page 2.

Place	Date	Hour	Summary of Events and Information	Remarks and references to Appendices
CHELMSFORD ½" O.S.	12/1/16		Company Instruction under 3rd ARMY Instructors. Lt CLARK sent to 182nd SIGNALS, DANBURY to instruct No 2 BDE. SECTION	C&B
CHELMSFORD ½" O.S.	13/1/16 — 16/1/16		Company Instruction. All transport thoroughly overhauled and inspected. Times of Parades altered and Stables at 7.0 p.m. instead of 8.0 p.m. from 16.1.16. Lectures to linesmen	C&B
CHELMSFORD ½" O.S.	17/1/16		Lectures on D.C. sets to Telegraph Operators. All transport wagons restocked and inspected by O.C.	C&B
CHELMSFORD ½" O.S.	18/1/16		Inspection by I.G.R.E. at BOREHAM. Court of Enquiry held on GE M.C. WHEELER'S bent motor cycle. MAJOR ALLAN President	C&B
CHELMSFORD ½" O.S.	19/1/16 — 22/1/16		Company Instruction. Small Signal Office schemes held for instructing H.Q. Signal Office staff. Lectures on diagram drawing to Telegraph Operators. Lt CLARK reported to O.C. No 4 BDE. SECTION at GREAT BADDOW. Cable repairing	C&B
CHELMSFORD ½" O.S.	23/1/16		2nd LIEUT. BROWNING reported to O.C. M.T. depôt BEDFORD for course of instruction in motor engines.	C&B
CHELMSFORD ½" O.S.	24/1/16 — 26/1/16		Linesmen lectures and special instruction in cable laying. Riding Instruction under SERGT- INSTRUCTOR BRYAN. Infantry drill. Cable repairing.	C&B

Army Form C. 2118

WAR DIARY
or
INTELLIGENCE SUMMARY
(Erase heading not required.)

51st SIGNALS R.E.   Page 3

Instructions regarding War Diaries and Intelligence Summaries are contained in F. S. Regs., Part II. and the Staff Manual respectively. Title Pages will be prepared in manuscript.

Place	Date	Hour	Summary of Events and Information	Remarks and references to Appendices
CHELMSFORD ½ O.S.	27/1/16		Instruction in cable laying. Lt CLARK reported to 183rd SIGNALS, BRENTWOOD to instruct No 3 BDE. SECTION	CRB
CHELMSFORD ½ O.S.	28/1/16 31/1/16		Course of instruction by Lt DICKSON finished 28/1/16. Instruction in cable laying carried on LIEUT WARE. All section instruments carefully overhauled and inspected by OC No1 SECTION Riding and Driving Instruction.	CRB

L.S. Heaven
O.C. 51st Div Sig Coy.

Appendix A

61st Divl. Signal Coy. R.E.
S C H E M E 11.1.16.

GENERAL IDEA.   An enemy Force is advancing on the line HIGH EASTER - PLESHEY - GREAT WALTHAM - HATFIELD PEVEREL.

The 61st DIV. will occupy and hold the line B in BROOMFIELD - BELSTEAD HALL - NEW HALL at 11.a.m.

The DIV. is disposed as follows:-

61st DIV.	100 yds S.E. of Railway Bridge. 500 N.W. of C in CHELMSFORD.
182nd BDE.	Rd. Junc. N.W. of B. in BROOMFIELD.
183rd BDE.	B in BELSTEAD HALL.
184th BDE.	E in NEW HALL.
C.R.A.	Mill S of E in CHELMSFORD.

PERSONNEL.

G.O.C. 61st DIV.	Capt. J. G. Heaven.
O.C. No.1 Section.	2nd Lieut. R.J. Ferguson.
O.C. 182nd BDE.	Sergt. Kemshaw.
O.C. 183rd BDE.	Corpl. Barton.
O.C. 184th BDE.	Sergt. Bryan.
C.R.A.	Corpl. Belmont.
Signal Master.	Sergt. Henderson.
Signal Clerk.	L/Cpl. Aspinall.
Asst. Signal Clerk.	L/Cpl. Colton.
Check.	Sapper Burton.
"	Driver Nash.
Despatch Rider.	Corpl. Duddridge.
" "	Sapper Aust.
" "	Pnr. Pearcey.

SECRET   Page 1

Army Form C. 2118.

WAR DIARY
or
INTELLIGENCE SUMMARY.
(Erase heading not required.)

61st Divl. Signal Company
Hdqrs & No 1 Section of
Month of May 1916

Instructions regarding War Diaries and Intelligence Summaries are contained in F. S. Regs., Part II. and the Staff Manual respectively. Title pages will be prepared in manuscript.

Place	Date 1916 May	Hour	Summary of Events and Information	Remarks and references to Appendices
CHOLDERTON	1st	6.15	Divisional Training	K.C.1
	12th		Inspection by H.M. The King on BULFORD FIELD	
	19th/19		Divisional Training	
	20th		Preparing for move to France	
	21st		Day fine. Time put forward 1 hour at 2 a.m. Paraded & marched to Tidworth Station. Commenced entraining 3.15 p.m. Train moved off 4.15 p.m. Arrived & disembarked 5.55 p.m. Embarked on S.S. North Western Miller. Sailed	
WARE	22nd		at 7.30 p.m. Arrived Havre about 4 a.m. Commenced disembarking about 1 p.m. (wings of field) Moved to No 5 Rest Camp about 3 p.m. Men and animals had good nights rest.	
	23rd		Day fine and bright.	
	25th		Paraded 11 a.m. moved off to Point 1 Havre Railway Siding. Commenced entraining about 12.15 p.m. & all difficulty with mules entraining. All on board by 1st Section	

WAR DIARY or INTELLIGENCE SUMMARY

Army Form C. 2118.

Page 2

(Erase heading not required.)

Place	Date	Hour	Summary of Events and Information	Remarks and references to Appendices
HAVRE	1916 May 23rd		Train moved off 2.47 p.m., 2 Coy Warwicks also on train, just stop at 10.15 p.m. Walked around a bit, and turned all men out with tea. Moved off 10.45 p.m.	
"	24th		Arrived Abbeyville about 3.15 a.m. Waited & fed and wired today's rations. Arrived NERVILLE about 1 p.m. Commenced detraining. Train clear by 1.30 p.m. Moved off to ST VENANT at 2 p.m. Horses and men billeted in a farm about 1½ miles from St VENANT (H.Q.s. Signal Office was wonderful quite near Rue Kulgrs, G.O.C., A.D.C., & G.S.O.) arrived 8 p.m. Day fine. Telephone Stores arrived from A.D.R. unpacked in morning. Arranged tent with 2d. Art. Hdqrs. during afternoon. Motor lorry and car arrived by road from HAVRE about 7 p.m. Car changed for a Wolseley at ABBEVILLE.	
ST VENANT	25th		1.82d B. de arrived about 4 p.m. at GONNEHEM. Went and in car and fixed up Visitor office there. Line also	

Page 3.

WAR DIARY or INTELLIGENCE SUMMARY.

Army Form C. 2118.

Place	Date	Hour	Summary of Events and Information	Remarks and references to Appendices
STIVERANT	1916 May 26/5		Day fine, got line to 2RB through temporarily. Party from APA coming out to repair it this morning. Sent Sgt. Kempshott and fay to Robec and LES LAURIERS to test lines to positions of other two A.dc's. Lines correct.	
"	"		Day fine. Conference at 3pm. all Corps Sadayrs under A.D.M.S. Major Butts. Several important forms were discussed. Met O.C. Signal Coys (incl. amy of 35th 33rd 37th 33rd and 61st Divisions) 183 Rd. arrived at ROBEC today.	
STIVENANT 27"	"		Day fine. Church Parade at Camp at 9.30 am. Took theodors + instrument over to LES LAURIERS and fitted up Office for 184th Brigade arriving today.	
"	28"		Day fine. Capn. Clark, Lt. Browning and Capn. Ralton went over to 33rd Div today, to look round communications. Lines to our Brigades not working at all well.	
"	29"		Major Butts came to visit us this evening. Our Signal Office staff getting rather more work than they could deal with.	

page 4.

Army Form C. 2118.

WAR DIARY
or
INTELLIGENCE SUMMARY.
(Erase heading not required.)

Instructions regarding War Diaries and Intelligence Summaries are contained in F. S. Regs., Part II. and the Staff Manual respectively. Title pages will be prepared in manuscript.

Place	Date	Hour	Summary of Events and Information	Remarks and references to Appendices
ST VENANT	1916 May 30th		Heavy rain during night but it cleared up at 9 am. Having finished of 9 am daily. After that, Horse exercise + riding drill. Sgt. Byron arrived today from 11th Corps to help in the Signal Office.	
"	31st		2nd Lieut Clarke to Bennett and Capt. Pearson head wires to 39th Division today to modify existing arrangements for communication. Lt. Tender + 10 other ranks at 39th Division for later round their Brigade Sections. H. Regnart 33rd Divn	

R. C. Pearson Capt.
O.C. 6th 1st Signal Coy

WAR DIARY
or
INTELLIGENCE SUMMARY

61st Signal Coy

Place	Date	Hour	Summary of Events and Information	Remarks and references to Appendices
In the field ST VENANT	1916 June 1st		Day fine. Cpl. Fitzhenry, L/C Dodd, and Sapper Walker sent to 39th Div. for three days instruction. Parties out clearing away branches of trees from the lines. Busy working out Signal Notes for the Staff.	
"	2nd		Day fine. 8 men of Cyclist Coy. attached to Sig. Coy. from XI Corps Hqrs. as Orderlies. Cpl. Williamson arrived from AAR for duty in the Signal Office. Four of our Officers visited 38th Div. Sigs. at LA GORGUE today. Signal Office working smoothly.	
"	3rd		Day fine. Nothing to report.	
"	4th		Day fine. Church Parade 9.30 am. Nothing to report.	
"	5th		Day fine. Visited 35th Div. Signals today at LESTREM	
"	6th		Heavy rain during night and this morning. Visited 117th Bde. of 39th Div. this afternoon. All correct in Signal Office and Nothing to report.	

www.ingramcontent.com/pod-product-compliance
Lightning Source LLC
Chambersburg PA
CBHW081511160426
43193CB00014B/2649